VOICE OF
THE PAIUTES

A Creative Minds Biography

VOICE OF THE PAIUTES

A Story about Sarah Winnemucca

by Jodie Shull

illustrations by Keith Birdsong

M Millbrook Press/Minneapolis

For my Nevada children, Barry and Kristina —J.S.

Millbrook Press, Inc.
A division of Lerner Publishing Group
241 First Avenue North
Minneapolis, MN 55401 U.S.A.

Website address: www.lernerbooks.com

Library of Congress Cataloging-in-Publication Data

Shull, Jodie A.
    Voice of the Paiutes : a story about Sarah Winnemucca / by Jodie Shull;
    illustrated by Keith Birdsong.
        p.   cm. — (A creative minds biography)
    Includes bibliographical references and index.
    ISBN-13: 978–0–8225–5990–0 (lib. bdg. : alk. paper)
    ISBN-10: 0–8225–5990–0 (lib. bdg. : alk. paper)
    1. Hopkins, Sarah Winnemucca, 1844?–1891—Juvenile literature.
    2. Paiute Indians—Biography—Juvenile literature. 3. Paiute Indians—
    History—Juvenile literature. I. Title. II. Series.
    E99.P2S48 2007
    979.004'9745769'0092—dc22   2005023741

Manufactured in the United States of America
1 2 3 4 5 6 – JR – 12 11 10 09 08 07

Table of Contents

Changed Forever   7

Sarah Finds Her Voice   13

Princess on Stage   22

We Want Peace   31

A Daring Rescue   38

Voice of the Paiutes   44

Sarah's Dream   54

Afterword   59

Selected Bibliography   61

Websites   61

Index   62

About the Author and Illustrator   64

Changed Forever

Seven-year-old Sarah clung to her brother's waist as they bounced along the rocky trail. She sat behind him as his horse made its way up the mountain path that led west to California. Her brother's rabbit fur blanket was wet with her tears. Sarah sobbed loudly. She hated her grandfather's plan to lead them into the heart of the white people's territory.

Sarah was terrified of white people. In her short life, she had seen the beginning of the white invasion of her high desert home. A few white settlers lived in the wilderness west of the Great Salt Lake and east of the Sierra Nevada.

More settlers were on the way. Sarah's people, the Northern Paiutes, had lived undisturbed for thousands of years. They knew the ways of the natural world and found the food and shelter they needed for survival.

Sarah's parents believed in hiding from the white settlers, but her grandfather had a different idea. He remembered an old legend about the return of the Paiutes' white brothers. It said the white brothers must be welcomed with friendship. When explorer John C. Frémont passed through the Paiute homeland, Sarah's grandfather joined him and traveled along to California. Frémont gave him the name Captain Truckee, meaning "very good," and wrote a letter for him to keep. Truckee called the letter his "rag friend" because it spoke to other white men about his service as a guide to the white leader.

Sarah loved her grandfather, but she could not share his faith in the white brothers. When she was born in 1844, only a few Paiutes had seen white people. From her people, Sarah heard stories that the white men looked like owls with their whiskery faces and large, round eyes.

Sarah's mother was Captain Truckee's daughter. Sarah's father was a powerful antelope hunter called Winnemucca. Sarah was her parents' fourth child and second daughter.

When Sarah was only four, she had a terrible experience. She and her mother were in a group of Paiutes gathering seeds in the open brush when a warning came. White hunters were approaching. Sarah's mother and her aunt began to run toward the hills, dragging their little children behind them. Sarah was too frightened and too small to run very far. Her desperate mother decided to hide Sarah and her young cousin and come back for them later.

Sarah found herself buried up to her chin in the sandy soil with her cousin beside her. A covering of sagebrush hid their faces and shaded them from the sun. The little girls must not make a sound, Mother said. She had heard stories that the white owls not only killed native people but also ate them. The two little girls waited all day—afraid to move or cry out. Finally, after nightfall, their mothers returned for them and lifted them from their sandy beds.

Three years later, in 1851, Sarah still had not forgotten her fear as she rode away from her desert home toward the unknown land of California. Captain Truckee wanted his family to spend the winter working for his white friends and learning their ways. The family traveled on horseback, camping each night, until they reached the town of Stockton, California, on the San Joaquin River. Sarah's mother coaxed her out of hiding to see the amazing, tall houses along the river and to taste the sweet food the white people called cake.

Soon afterward, Sarah became very sick. Her mother thought the white people's cake had poisoned her. Sarah's eyes swelled shut, and she ached and itched all over. A friendly white woman visited their camp and smeared Sarah with some medicine that eased her pain. Sarah had touched poison oak on the trip over the mountains. This strange plant was not known to the desert Paiutes. The white lady's kindness gave Sarah a new feeling. As her grandfather said, there was good in the white world.

Captain Truckee guided his family down the river to visit the ranch of his friend Hiram Scott. Here Sarah spent her first night inside a wooden house with a roof. She was used to the simple wickiup, a hut made of brush and matting. Sarah saw her first table and chairs. She was fascinated by the red upholstered chairs in the dining room. She waited her turn to sit in one of the beautiful chairs. When she took her place at the table, she was so excited that she almost forgot to eat.

During that mild winter in the Sierra foothills, Sarah first heard the English and Spanish languages. Her grandfather and brothers were given a small herd of horses for their work at the ranch.

The Paiute family returned to the desert when spring came. Sarah had seen many wonderful things. Her grandfather's confidence in the goodness of his white brothers remained strong. Sarah realized that his stories about the white people's power were true. The white people had wonders, and they were powerful. But what were they going to do with their power?

When Sarah's family returned to the desert, they found that many of the Paiute people had died that winter from a mysterious illness. The Paiute leaders insisted that the white settlers had poisoned the river they used for drinking water. Captain Truckee tried to calm them. A poisoned river would kill everyone who drank from it, he explained, including the white settlers. Truckee blamed the deaths on a fearsome disease, new to the Paiutes. The disease was cholera, which spread in the water that flowed from mining camps.

The Paiutes grieved for their dead and turned to the summer's work of finding food and building shelters. Sarah's father and grandfather disagreed over how to live in the presence of white people. Whether the Paiutes ran from the white brothers or tried to learn their ways, their way of life was changed forever.

Sarah Finds Her Voice

In the years that followed Sarah's winter stay in California, the stream of white travelers across her desert homeland became a flood. Ranchers, farmers, traders, and prospectors in search of gold and silver followed the Humboldt and Carson rivers west. They claimed the land, the water, and the wildlife that had once meant survival for the Paiutes. Sarah's people had always lived by roaming the land with the seasons, looking for sources of food. The white settlers were different. They built houses, barns, and trading posts. They fenced the land and dammed the rivers, shaping the natural world to their needs.

The Paiutes watched as more and more of their resources vanished. Still, Sarah's grandfather stood firm in his belief that the white brothers must be accepted in peace and friendship. Survival would come from learning their ways. In the spring of Sarah's thirteenth year, Captain Truckee asked a family of white settlers to take Sarah and her little sister, Elma, into their home.

Major William Ormsby and his wife, Margaret, had just moved east over the mountains from California. They made their home in the small village of Genoa in the eastern shadow of the towering Sierra Nevada. Sarah and Elma went to live with the Ormsbys in a cabin inside an old log fort called Mormon Station. Nine-year-old Lizzie Ormsby enjoyed having two young playmates around the house. Living with a white family, the bright and eager Sarah learned to speak English very well.

She watched the daily life of the little town with amazement. Soon she knew the names of all the families who settled along the Carson River. From Lizzie's mother, Sarah and Elma learned to sew and keep house. They may also have shared Lizzie's lessons in reading and writing. From those days on, Sarah continued to educate herself. She especially wanted to learn the powerful skill of "talking on paper."

Sarah was happy, even though she missed her parents and their summertime camp at Pyramid Lake. Perhaps her grandfather was right, and the Paiutes could live in peace beside the white brothers. Then, in September 1857, an event she would never forget rocked Sarah's peaceful world. Two white traders carrying supplies over the mountains from California were murdered. No one knew what had happened. Arrows, American Indian weapons, were found at the scene.

Major Ormsby sent for Sarah's older brother Natches. Natches was the Paiutes' peace chief. His job was to bring any wrongdoers among his people to justice. The arrows from the murder scene belonged to the nearby Washo tribe. Natches asked the Washo chief to find the murderers and turn them in. The Washo chief protested that none of his people could be guilty. Major Ormsby insisted that the arrows proved otherwise. He told the chief to find the murderers or face the anger of the white settlers.

Six days later, Sarah and Elma stood by the dusty road that passed through Genoa. They watched with all the residents of the tiny village as the Washo chief brought three young men to the fort. The men's mothers and sisters followed, crying. The chief had chosen these three men to bring to Major Ormsby because they were young and had no children to feed. The terrified men tried to run away. Shots rang out, and the men fell to the ground.

Sarah was horrified. She knew she must speak out. She ran sobbing to Mrs. Ormsby. "I believe those Washo women," she cried. "They say their men are all innocent. They were not away from their camp for a long time." Mrs. Ormsby stared at Sarah. Major Ormsby was in charge, she told Sarah, and he knew the right thing to do.

Sarah watched with helpless sorrow as the Washos grieved for their dead. "I thought my heart would break," she said. She would never forget this terrible example of the white brothers' justice. Little Elma fell sick soon after witnessing the deaths of the Washo men. Sarah and Elma stayed on at the Ormsby home only long enough for Elma to get well. Then they returned to their family. Sarah took with her all that she had learned—her skill in English and a frightening vision of what conflicts her people might face in the years to come.

Sarah's people had many homes. They gathered in spring to fish on the Truckee River. In the fall, they traveled to the Pine Nut Mountains to gather the seeds of the piñon pine trees. Paiute families scattered across the high desert and followed the ways of their ancestors. Traveling across the land was becoming more difficult and dangerous for the Paiutes. White settlers moved into the best of their gathering and hunting places. Like the antelope and coyotes, the Paiutes had to move out of the way to survive.

Some Paiutes could find work in white homes and on nearby ranches. For a time, Sarah lived with her older sister, Mary, and brother Natches near a mining settlement called Johnstown. The time she spent living near and working for white people helped Sarah learn more about the strange new society that was growing up around her.

She taught herself to speak English almost as perfectly as the white people themselves. She joined in town activities and attended some of the Saturday dances held at the local saloon. A newspaper man reported that "Miss Sarah Winnemucca, the Paiute Princess" was asked to join the dancing. Sarah's family was well known to the white settlers. Because her grandfather was a Paiute leader, they thought that "princess" seemed like a good title for the charming young Sarah.

Winter was always a dangerous season for the Paiutes. The high altitude of their homeland brought fierce winds and freezing temperatures. Without warm clothing, strong shelters, and a good supply of stored seeds and dried meat, the people could not survive. Sarah's father took his family to California during the very harsh winter of 1858–1859. They fished and hunted in the mild San Joaquin valley. Wherever she traveled, Sarah continued to gain knowledge. In California she may have learned both the Spanish language and the art of Mexican folk dancing.

The following winter brought even worse cold and heavy snows. The Paiutes suffered many deaths from freezing and starvation. When the weather was harsh, the foods of the desert became scarce. There was not enough to support the growing human population. While the white settlers took more and more land, the native people grew poorer and hungrier. Peace and friendship depended on enough food and land for all. Some Paiutes believed that they would soon have to fight or starve.

In 1859 a rich vein of silver and gold, called the Comstock Lode, was discovered in the mountains south of Pyramid Lake. The promise of wealth brought another wave of white settlers into the Paiute homeland. Fear and distrust grew between the Paiutes and the settlers. When the Paiutes gathered in 1860 for spring fishing at Pyramid Lake, the leaders talked together. Some believed war against the white invaders was their only choice. Sarah's cousin

Numaga spoke out for peace. He told his people that there were as many white men as there were grains of sand in the riverbed or the stars in the sky. How could the Paiutes hope to win?

Conflicts between the white settlers and the Paiutes grew. In May 1860, a small band of white volunteer soldiers attacked a group of Paiutes near Pyramid Lake. The Paiutes won the small battle, driving the whites back to the town of Virginia City. Where could the Paiutes turn for justice? Who would listen to their side of the story? The white settlers called upon the U.S. government to protect them. The U.S. Army began to track the Paiutes as they fled into the desert north of Pyramid Lake.

The Pyramid Lake War of 1860 was the first of many battles to come. A period of peace came in the fall of 1860, when Sarah was sixteen. The government promised the Paiutes a reservation, an area of land reserved only for them, at Pyramid Lake. Hopes were high. Then, in October, word came that Sarah's beloved grandfather Truckee was dying. Paiutes gathered in the Pine Nut Mountains to honor him.

Truckee named Sarah's father, Winnemucca, the new head chief and told him to be a good father to his people. Truckee asked that Sarah and Elma be sent to school in California. Sarah sat by Truckee, afraid to leave his side. "I think if he had put out his hands and asked me to go with him," she said, "I would gladly have folded myself in his arms." Sarah's courageous spirit and eagerness to learn came from her grandfather. She followed his path of peace and remembered the power of his "rag friend."

3

Princess on Stage

Sarah's brothers honored their grandfather's wish to take their sisters to California to go to school. Sadly, Sarah and Elma were able to attend for only a few weeks. In those times, parents of white students did not want American Indian girls attending their school. Though Sarah's feelings were hurt, she kept up with her studies on her own. Everything that she learned and experienced gave her more strength. She could speak English, Spanish, and three different Native American languages. She could also read and write English quite well. And she was an excellent horseback rider, seamstress, and cook.

Sarah knew the traditions and survival skills of her people as well as the ways of white society. She grew up with a place in two worlds, though it was not always comfortable to move back and forth between them. What she saw in these worlds could be painful and frightening.

Each year the Paiutes grew poorer and hungrier. Many of them lived on reservations. Forced to live in one place, the Paiutes could not search for food in their traditional way. Government agents hired to take care of the American Indians were often dishonest. They sold the food and clothing they were supposed to give the American Indians to white settlers.

In September 1864, Sarah's father, Chief Winnemucca, decided to ask the white settlers themselves for help. He would plead for donations of money to buy the food and blankets his people needed to survive the winter. Chief Winnemucca, one son, and two daughters, including twenty-year-old Sarah, rode through the streets of Virginia City. When a crowd gathered to see them, Winnemucca began to speak. Sarah translated his words. The Paiute men, women, and children were starving, he said. On the reservation, they could not travel to hunt wild animals or search for plants to eat. Winnemucca collected only twenty-five dollars for his people.

That trip was the beginning of Sarah's role as a speaker and performer for her people. The Winnemucca family came to town again with a small party of warriors riding behind their chief. Sarah rode beside her father. Winnemucca told the curious crowd that the Paiutes were determined to live in peace, even though other tribes might oppose them for it. Sarah translated. She also made sure local newspapers had stories to publish about her people and their troubles.

Soon the family made their plea on stage. Wealthy Virginia City had a theater where traveling opera singers and Shakespearean actors performed. Before the chief gave his speech, the Winnemucca family presented a series of tableaus—scenes from Paiute life in which the actors stood perfectly still. Sarah had an attack of stage fright the first time she tried to translate with theater lights shining in her eyes. She sat down and covered her face with her hands. "I'm so ashamed! I can't tell you what Winnemucca is saying." The crowd applauded just the same, and the show was a great success.

In hopes of reaching a larger audience, the family took their performance to San Francisco, California. On October 22, 1864, the Metropolitan Theater presented "Winnemucca, Chief of the Paiutes." The performance included his two daughters and eight warriors. The theater used forest scenery that looked nothing like the Paiutes' desert home. Sarah and her family wore costumes made of deerskin, not the rabbit skin of Paiute custom. White audiences in big cities expected all native people to look like the warriors of the American plains. News stories praised Sarah's "sweet English voice" and the Paiutes' amazing ability to stand as still as statues in their show.

Sarah's experience on stage taught her how to capture the interest of an audience. She learned to move and speak without fear. Unfortunately, the family's trip to San Francisco cost more than they collected in donations. They returned home weary and discouraged. Nevada, where the Paiutes lived, became the country's thirty-sixth state in 1864, but little changed for Sarah's struggling people.

In March 1865, violence broke out between the Paiutes and the white settlers. Fear on both sides made any crime an act of war. After Paiutes killed two white men, a troop of volunteer soldiers attacked a Paiute camp at Mud Lake. All the men from the camp had gone hunting. The soldiers killed everyone left at the camp, including Sarah's mother and baby brother. Sarah's sister Mary escaped by riding away on her father's fastest horse.

Overcome by sorrow, Chief Winnemucca retreated to the wilderness of southern Oregon. The Mud Lake Massacre was the beginning of a white campaign to kill or capture all of the much-feared American Indians. Sarah had only her words to express her grief and outrage. "They went after my people all over Nevada," she later wrote in her autobiography. She blamed the violence on reports by white settlers that the Paiutes were stealing from them. "The trail began which is marked by the blood of my people from hill to hill and from valley to valley," she wrote.

The Paiutes and the neighboring Bannock and Shoshone tribes needed to steal food or they would starve. Governor Henry G. Blasdel of Nevada visited the American Indian camps in 1866 and found the people eating rabbits, mice, grasshoppers, and ants. White settlers had cut down their piñon pine forests and grazed cattle on the grasses that once provided seeds for food. A government agent estimated that half of all the Paiutes had died from starvation, disease, and warfare between 1859 and 1865.

Sarah spent the winter of 1866 living with Natches and his family on the Pyramid Lake Reservation. What she saw there started her lifelong fight against the injustices of the reservation system. Because she could speak excellent English, she challenged the reservation agents who cheated her people and lied to them. She went to the newspapers to tell her story. Already respected as the daughter of Chief Winnemucca, Sarah quickly became known for her outspoken ways.

In 1868 a dishonest reservation agent sold gunpowder to one of the Paiutes. Later, the Paiute was killed when he was caught with the illegal gunpowder. His family wanted justice for the cruel trick. The reservation agent called for help from the U.S. Army. Sarah was amazed and grateful that the army commander became an unexpected source of help for her people. He decided to hear the Paiutes' side of the story before deciding what to do.

Sarah and Natches rode with a party of twenty Paiute warriors to a meeting with army officers. Sarah's passionate words and flashing black eyes convinced them that her version of the story was true. The army ordered three wagonloads of food for the Paiutes and asked Sarah and Natches to bring Chief Winnemucca and his followers to stay at the army's Camp McDermit. Sarah realized then that her people would be safer and better fed in the care of the army than they were on the reservation. By 1869 Sarah was working for the army as a translator because of her excellent English.

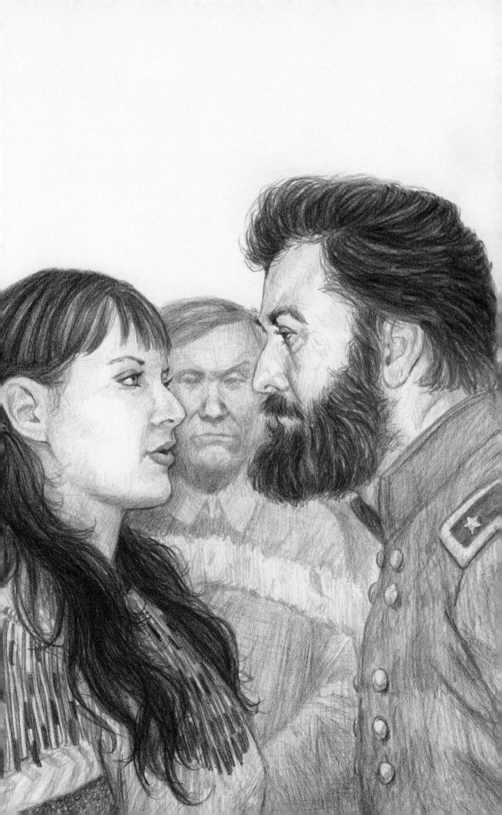

Holding a job with the U.S. government separated Sarah from her people. Some did not understand her efforts and called her a traitor. But Sarah remembered the advice of her grandfather. Keeping peace was the only hope for the Paiutes. Those who chose to fight the white brothers would not survive.

4

We Want Peace

In 1870, when Sarah was twenty-six years old, she wrote an important letter. The commander at the Camp McDermit army post asked her to explain in detail the poor condition of her people to the Nevada government. Her graphic letter described the terrible suffering of the Paiutes and the unfair treatment on the reservation. The letter was so good that Nevada officials sent it on to Washington, D.C. Several newspapers and *Harper's* magazine printed the letter for the public to read. Sarah's powerful words reached readers across the country.

In her letter, Sarah explained what a reservation should provide for her people. They needed a permanent home on their native land. They needed education so they could learn how to make a living and live in peace with their white neighbors. They needed safety and protection from white settlers who ignored reservation borders. At Pyramid Lake, white farmers and ranchers had taken over the best reservation land and invaded the Paiute fishing grounds. Living on the reservation, Sarah's people were trapped and starving. Reservation agents gave them few supplies and little help of any kind.

Sarah and the other Paiutes living at the Camp McDermit army post had better care. They were given food, clothing, and protection. But Sarah knew the army could not take care of the Paiutes forever. At the army camp, Sarah moved back and forth between two cultures. She worked for the white soldiers, but she also lived the life of her people—dancing, riding horses, and joining the women for noisy games of Paiute football.

Sarah never stopped using her quick wit and sharp tongue to speak out against injustice. Without fear, she criticized government officials. Because she spoke out, she made powerful enemies in her fight for fair treatment. In 1873 a reporter from the *Nevada*

State Journal newspaper invited "the Paiute Princess" to tell her story. She gave the reporter a history of her people and a list of the problems they faced. She voiced her anger at reservation agents who sold food supplies and farming tools meant for the Paiutes and took bribes from white ranchers for the use of reservation land.

Although she felt great anger, Sarah tried to be a peacemaker. She knew the conflict between American Indians and white settlers in the land of the Great Basin was not over. The Modoc and Bannock peoples to the north were preparing for war. Sarah warned her people not to join a hopeless fight that would kill many and bring more harm to their way of life. In 1874 Sarah traveled to San Francisco with her father and her brothers Natches and Tom. They visited the highest military commander in the western United States and asked for guarantees of help for the starving Paiutes. They spoke out for their people but returned to Nevada empty-handed.

In 1875 Sarah rode north to Camp Harney, an army post in southeastern Oregon. She went there to join her father and other family members for a traditional springtime gathering on the safe ground of the camp. The vast Malheur Reservation stretched to the east of Camp Harney. It was set aside in 1872 for American

Indians of the region who were willing to live there. Malheur had water, good farmland, and abundant wildlife. While Sarah was visiting Camp Harney, her half brother, Lee, brought her a message. The reservation agent wanted Sarah to come to Malheur and work for him.

Sarah had not had good experiences working on reservations. This time, however, things were different. She discovered that Malheur's agent, Sam Parrish, was a good and honest man who wanted to help the American Indian people survive. He planned to teach them how to farm and grow the food they needed. He also planned to build a school. Sarah and many of the Paiute people responded with gratitude to the new hope Parrish offered them. They worked hard building fences and an irrigation ditch to channel water to their crops.

Sarah served as an interpreter for Sam Parrish. When the new school was finally finished, she became an assistant teacher. Sarah discovered that she loved teaching. She was able to use the Paiute children's native language to help them learn English. "They learned very fast, and were glad to come to school," she later wrote. "I cannot tell or express how happy we were!" The happiness of the Paiutes did not last, however.

White ranchers wanted some of the western lands at the Malheur Reservation. Sam Parrish opposed the takeover of reservation land. The white ranchers managed to have Parrish fired. The new agent at Malheur was as cruel as Parrish had been kind. He told the Paiutes that reservation land belonged to the government and not to them. They were ordered to turn over their food crops to him. Those who refused were told to leave the reservation.

Sarah and her father opposed the new agent and tried to get help from the army. The new agent fired Sarah from her teaching job. Many of the Paiutes left the reservation to seek shelter in the nearby mountains. Their hopes for a safe home were gone. To the east, another band of native people, the Bannocks, were ready to challenge the white brothers. Like the Paiutes, they had suffered hunger, hardship, and false promises on their reservation. The Bannocks decided to die fighting. They invited the Paiutes to join them.

In the spring of 1878, Chief Winnemucca and Natches visited the Bannock camp to plead for peace. They showed the warriors two piles of sand on the ground. A large pile represented the white soldiers and a tiny one represented the native people. The Bannocks refused to listen. At the same time, Sarah was driving her wagon and team of horses east toward

Idaho. She was ready to travel to Washington, D.C., to find the president and ask him to help her people. Before she reached the train station, she learned that the Bannock War had begun. Her trip to the East would have to wait. Sarah was in danger. Rumors spread that the Bannocks were hoping to capture Chief Winnemucca's daughter. Although Sarah didn't know it at the time, many Paiutes, including her father, were already being held as prisoners in the Bannock camp.

5

A Daring Rescue

The army commander asked for volunteers to track the Bannock war party and bring back information about their movements. Because of the great danger, none of the Paiute scouts wanted to go. They had heard that Sarah's brother Natches had been killed while helping some white men escape from the Bannocks. Sarah was grief-stricken. "My heart was dead within me," she wrote. Sarah knew that she must volunteer to serve the U.S. Army. Fighting the white brothers would only end in more suffering. An early peace would save many lives, and Sarah could help.

The army needed scouts and guides who knew the land and the ways of the native people. Sarah turned her grief into action and offered to go on the dangerous mission to find the Bannocks' camp. If she found any Paiutes at the camp, she would help them escape. "There is nothing that will stop me," said Sarah.

Sarah chose a good horse to ride and asked for a "rag friend" similar to one her grandfather had carried. A letter from the army would protect her from any hostile white settlers she might meet. With two other Paiute scouts, Sarah rode one hundred miles through the wilderness, tracking the Bannock warriors. On the slope of Steens Mountain, Sarah met her half brother, Lee, who told her both good and bad news.

The good news was that Natches was alive. He had escaped from the Bannocks. The bad news was that Chief Winnemucca and his band were prisoners in the Bannock camp, without guns, horses, or blankets. They had no way to defend themselves from the Bannocks or the U.S. Army. Sarah had a plan. She would sneak into the enemy camp to find her father and persuade him to run from the Bannocks.

Sarah had made the long ride to Steens Mountain in southeastern Oregon in the clothes of a white woman. She would have to take off her hat and dress, unbraid her hair, and wrap a blanket around her to pass unnoticed into the camp. Sarah and Lee struggled up the steep mountainside, sometimes on horseback and sometimes crawling on their hands and knees. When they reached the crest of the mountain, they could see the large camp below.

For a moment, Sarah's fear mixed with pride as she looked down at the village of more than three hundred dwellings. It was the largest gathering of American Indians Sarah had ever seen. She and Lee crept into the Bannock camp. Lee knew the way to Chief Winnemucca's lodge. Her father was amazed and overjoyed to see Sarah. She quickly told him her escape plan. Once the Paiutes left the Bannock camp, General Oliver Howard had promised to give them protection.

Chief Winnemucca agreed to Sarah's plan. The Paiute women and children would leave the camp, pretending to gather wood. The men would follow when darkness fell. Lee was sent to steal as many horses as he could from the Bannock pasture and drive them down the mountainside. At dusk, Sarah and her father climbed the mountainside above the camp. Exhausted from her long ride and weak from hunger, fear, and lack of sleep, Sarah welcomed her father's strong hand pulling her along.

The Paiutes reached their horses and rode south as fast as they could travel. The small children rode tied to their mothers' backs. Soon the Bannocks discovered their escape and began to follow. Sarah and Lee's wife, Mattie, raced ahead to the army camp to ask for soldiers to come and escort the Paiutes to safety.

General Howard sent troops to the rescue. He reported that Sarah had saved more than seventy-five of her people. She continued to serve General Howard as a guide, interpreter, and scout during the remaining months of the war. "She did our government great service," Howard wrote. He praised Sarah for "all she willingly did to help the white settlers and her own people to live peaceably together."

At the war's end, all the American Indians in the army's custody were gathered at Camp Harney in southern Oregon. Among them were both Sarah's people who had remained peaceful and some who had joined the fighting. Sarah found herself in the middle of a terrible conflict. Orders came from Washington, D.C., for all the American Indians to move to the Yakima Reservation across the Columbia River far to the north in what became the state of Washington. Sarah had promised the Paiutes a safe home in their native territory. "My people have not done anything and why should they be sent away from their own country [in the lands around Nevada]?" she asked. Like her people, Sarah was a victim of the government's false promises. "My people will never believe me again," she wrote.

Sarah helped as many Paiute families as possible sneak away from the army camp into the mountains. She stayed behind to make the long journey with those who could not escape. More than five hundred men, women, and children were driven 350 miles over rugged, snowy mountains. They arrived at Yakima on February 2, 1879, exhausted, freezing, their clothing in rags. Sarah raged over the cruel decision to remove her people from their homeland. "What can the president be thinking?" Sarah asked. "Tell me, what is he? Is he man or beast?" Sarah would soon find out for herself.

6

Voice of the Paiutes

While she was at the Yakima Reservation, Sarah continued to fight for justice. She tried to help her people adjust to the strange land and climate. Yakima was north of the mighty Columbia River. The reservation was wetter and colder than the Paiutes' desert homeland. The Yakima people did not welcome the newcomers to their reservation. There was not enough food and clothing to go around. The Yakimas showed their resentment by stealing the few horses the Paiutes had left. Sarah lost her beloved horse too. The Paiutes were homesick and freezing. Many of them became ill and died.

Sarah tried to comfort her people and give them hope. She wrote to Natches back in Nevada and asked him to send her as many piñon nuts as he could spare. The familiar food would make good medicine for the Paiutes.

The reservation agent was like the others Sarah had rebelled against. He did not understand the needs of the people in his care. Sarah taught school for a short time and kept up her argument with the government. She would find a way to get her people back to their beloved homeland.

For weapons, she had only her strong will and her powerful voice. She started her campaign with a series of lectures in San Francisco in November 1879. Sarah was thirty-five years old. In the fifteen years since her last appearance on stage, her faith in herself and her beliefs had grown. She had knowledge and experience. People knew her name, and audiences in San Francisco were eager to see and hear her.

Sarah stepped proudly into the light, her waist-length black hair and her black eyes shining. As usual, she wore a deerskin dress decorated with fringe and beads. Sarah also wore red leather leggings and leather moccasins. This time there were no painted pine trees rising behind her or pantomime scenes of Paiute life.

Sarah told stories about her people, their legends, and beliefs. She entertained the audience with stories of her childhood and her adventures in the Bannock War. Sarah could make people laugh and cry. Tears fell from her eyes too, as she made her plea, "I am crying out to you for justice." At the heart of Sarah's message was the shame she heaped on the dishonest reservation agents and the government that gave power to such men.

Newspapers printed Sarah's challenge and finally the government had to answer her. In January 1880, Sarah, Natches, and Chief Winnemucca traveled across the country by train to visit Washington, D.C. Sarah had been invited to meet with Secretary of the Interior Carl Schurz, the highest official in charge of Indian policy. Sarah told Carl Schurz the story of the Bannock War. Then she translated for Natches while he pleaded for the release of the Paiute people in exile at Yakima.

Secretary Schurz signed a paper for Sarah giving permission for the Paiutes to return to their home country. Sarah and her family rejoiced. Nothing else in their Washington visit could compare with that happy achievement. When Sarah met with President Rutherford B. Hayes, he asked her if she had received what she wanted for her people. She replied, "Yes, sir, as far as I know."

Newspaper reports of Sarah's success reached Nevada before she did. When the family arrived at the train station in the town of Winnemucca, they found an enthusiastic crowd of people waiting to greet them.

Sarah waited until the end of April for the worst of the winter snow to melt. Then she began the long and difficult ride north to Yakima, carrying the joyful news to her people. When she arrived, she first visited the reservation agent to be sure he had received instructions from Washington. The agent said he knew nothing and grew angry when Sarah showed him her "beautiful letter." The Paiutes were eager to see Sarah's letter and danced with joy when she read it to them.

Sarah hoped her people would be allowed to depart that summer. Unfortunately, the Yakima agent and other government officials persuaded Secretary Schurz to change his order. They argued that it would be too dangerous for the Paiutes to return to their homeland. The travelers might face conflict with white settlers along the way. Without Sarah stirring up trouble, the agent wrote, the Paiutes would be happy to stay at Yakima forever. Sarah was heartbroken. Once again, she had carried false promises to her people.

Although the agent forced her to leave Yakima Reservation, she promised to keep fighting for justice. Sarah moved to nearby Fort Vancouver. There she worked as an interpreter and schoolteacher while sending messages of hope to her people at Yakima. She encouraged them not to give up their dreams of returning home.

While Sarah kept up her stream of letters to the government, small groups of Paiutes began to make their escape from Yakima. Families disappeared into the mountains and began the journey south on secret wilderness trails. They traveled unseen by the white settlers of the region until all the Paiutes had left Yakima. Less than half of the Paiutes who were sent to Yakima lived to return home, however. They had died from sickness, cold, and the lack of food.

In the spring of 1883, Sarah traveled east once again. This time she did not go directly to the government offices in Washington, D.C. Instead, she took her message to the people of the U.S. cities of the East. During the following year, Sarah gave more than three hundred speeches in Boston, New York, Philadelphia, Baltimore, and other cities. Large crowds flocked to see her and hear her strong words about her people's desperate struggle to survive.

In Boston, Sarah met two extraordinary women who became her close friends and helpers. Elizabeth Peabody and Mary Mann were elderly sisters who had devoted their lives to charity and education. The sisters encouraged Sarah to write a book about her people. With their help, Sarah completed *Life among the Paiutes: Their Wrongs and Claims*. Sarah's book told the story of her life and gave a history of the Paiute people and their culture. Mary Mann acted as Sarah's editor, and Elizabeth Peabody worked to get the book printed.

Published in 1883, Sarah's book was the first one written by an American Indian woman. Sarah's book was a powerful tool—like the "rag friend" that her grandfather had cherished years before. Words on paper carried Sarah's message to readers everywhere. Her knowledge of both the white and native cultures could promote understanding among people who had never met. She had also recorded the story of her people for future generations. Although the Paiutes would have to join white society to survive, she did not want their heritage and culture to disappear.

During the year that she lectured in the East, Sarah found many supporters for her cause. She collected thousands of signatures on a petition calling for the Paiutes to be allowed to return to their homeland.

In the spring of 1884, Sarah returned to Washington, D.C., to present her petition to the U.S. Congress. Sarah first visited the new president, Chester Arthur, and his secretary of the interior to look for any change of heart in the white leaders. They disappointed her once again. So Sarah took her cause to Congress and was invited to speak. After telling the story of her people, she asked only that they be returned to a safe home on the land where they were born. Sarah received sympathy—but no promises. Not knowing what the future held for her people, Sarah boarded a train headed west in the summer of 1884.

7

Sarah's Dream

Sarah returned to Pyramid Lake, Nevada. The deep blue desert lake had always been a sacred gathering place for her people. Many Paiutes—though poor, ragged, and hungry—still lived near the lake, clinging to the land.

Sarah had been promised a teaching position on the Pyramid Lake Reservation. Remembering her happy days as a teacher, Sarah hoped to heal her sorrows with useful work. She believed that reading and writing were the keys to the white brothers' power. Her own power to reach out with words had helped her people many times.

She wanted her people to have that power. "My people have been signing papers for the last twenty-three years," she wrote. "They don't know what they sign." If her people could speak the white brothers' language, they could tell their story and be heard.

Sarah did not receive her teaching job at Pyramid Lake. A new government agent wanted to give the job to one of his friends or relatives. Disappointed but not very surprised, Sarah decided to pursue a dream of her own. Her friend Elizabeth Peabody had sometimes conducted classes in her home. Miss Peabody encouraged Sarah to open her own school if she possibly could. Sarah knew she would need some money and a good location for her school.

Sarah gathered all her resources. She gave lectures in nearby towns. Miss Peabody sent her money from the sale of her book and from donations by friends Sarah had made in the East. Natches had managed to buy some land of his own near the small farming town of Lovelock, Nevada. Here Sarah opened her school for Paiute children in the summer of 1885. They could not afford a building for the school, so Sarah, Natches, and their friends made a canopy of sagebrush to shelter students from the blazing sun. Sarah's school was something completely new.

N
CANADA
MONTANA
WASHINGTON
Snake R.
ambia R.
16
15
11.
4
3
OREGON
6
5
ORNIA
NEV

In 1885 many American Indian children were being taken from their families and sent to live at distant boarding schools. They were forced to speak only English and told to forget that they were American Indians. The government thought this would be the best way to help native people become part of American society. But Sarah wanted to honor her people's culture by using their own language to teach English.

In the first year, Sarah's twenty-four students ranged in age from six to sixteen. Sarah named objects in the Paiute language and then taught her students the English names and spelling. They sat on the dirt floor and used their benches for desks to practice writing. The students played games, drew pictures, and also studied farming and housekeeping. Sarah used love and laughter to teach her students. She encouraged them to take their lessons home and help their parents learn too. Sarah provided food and clothing for her students when she could. Years later, they remembered her as a wonderful teacher.

Sarah called her school the Peabody Institute after her good friend in Boston. Miss Peabody sent all the donations she could gather for the school, but financial worries continued for Sarah and Natches. Their ranch needed a well to provide water, and the school would need a building in order to stay open during the freezing months of winter. Sarah was finally able to pay for a small schoolhouse, but the problem of water for the ranch remained. Without a sure supply of water, the ranch and school could not survive.

Sarah managed to keep her school open for almost four years. She and Miss Peabody asked repeatedly for government support. Many visitors came to the school and sent back excellent reports of Sarah's work and the children's progress. But official government recognition and financial help for the school never came. By the end of the summer of 1889, Sarah and Natches could not afford to keep both the ranch and the school going any longer.

Sick, exhausted, and discouraged, Sarah went to visit her sister Elma in Henry's Lake, Idaho. There, Sarah died of an unknown illness on October 16, 1891. She was forty-seven years old. Sarah was buried on a hillside near Henry's Lake. On October 27, news of Sarah's death appeared on the front page of the *New York Times* newspaper, an honor given to famous Americans. The title of Sarah's story read: "Princess Winnemucca Dead: The Most Remarkable Woman Among the Paiutes of Nevada." Sarah's battle for peace and justice was over, but her words and the work she had done for her people would live on.

Afterword

In October 2004, a young sculptor named Victor Benjamin was finishing work on a special project at the Nevada State Library. He had been chosen to make a statue of Sarah Winnemucca. Sarah's statue would be a gift to the National Statuary Hall in Washington, D.C. Benjamin smoothed the clay fingers of Sarah's right hand. In her outstretched hand, he shaped a flower. Sarah's Paiute name was Thocmetony, "Shell Flower." Benjamin said, "the flower is a symbol for peace, which was the goal of her life. . . ." In her left hand, she holds a book. Benjamin explained that since "she was the first Native American to write a book, . . . this was a good icon [symbol] for Sarah." Her hair and dress look swept by the wind, a symbol for change. Benjamin had studied Sarah's life carefully before designing her statue. He read her autobiography as well as books about her. He wanted to capture Sarah's spirit of courage and determination.

More than one hundred years after her death, Sarah Winnemucca has returned to Washington. She is the first Native American to be honored with a statue in the National Statuary Hall. Many of the causes Sarah fought for in her lifetime are being won. She fought for her people's right to peace, freedom, and justice. She fought for education that preserved her people's culture and language while helping them adapt to white society. Because of her writing, the history of her people and their struggles will never be forgotten. When Sarah spoke of her people, she also spoke of her own heart. "They know what love means," she wrote. "They are brave and will not be imposed upon." Sarah knew that peace depended on justice for all.

Selected Bibliography

Canfield, Gae Whitney. *Sarah Winnemucca of the Northern Paiutes*. Norman, OK: University of Oklahoma Press, 1983.

Hopkins, Sarah Winnemucca. *Life among the Piutes: Their Wrongs and Claims*. Reno, NV: University of Nevada Press, 1994.

Morrison, Dorothy Nafus. *Chief Sarah: Sarah Winnemucca's Fight for Indian Rights*. New York: Atheneum, 1980.

Scordato, Ellen. *Sarah Winnemucca: Northern Paiute Writer and Diplomat*. New York: Chelsea House, 1992.

Zanjani, Sally. *Sarah Winnemucca*. Lincoln: University of Nebraska Press, 2001.

Websites

National Women's Hall of Fame
http://greatwomen.org
Look for Sarah Winnemucca among America's great women.

Nevada State Library and Archives
http://dmla.clan.lib.nv.us/docs/nsla/Winnemucca/SarahWinnemucca.htm
See photos of Sarah's statue.

Sarah Winnemucca Elementary School
http://www.Washoe.k12.nv.us/winnemucca
Visit the Nevada school named for Sarah and read more about her life.

Index

Arthur, Chester, 53

Bannock people, 27; in camp, 39–40; preparing for war, 33, 36, 37, 38
Bannock War, 37, 38
Benjamin, Victor, 59
Blasdel, Henry G., 27

Camp Harney, Oregon, 33, 42
Camp McDermit, Nevada, 28, 31, 32
Captain Truckee (grandfather), 7, 8, 9; confidence in white brothers, 12; courageous spirit of, 21; death of, 20–21; message of peace, 21, 30, 51
Comstock Lode, 19
Congress, the U.S., 53

disease, 27, 50

food and shelter, 8, 12, 13, 17, 18–19, 22, 23, 27, 28, 34, 50
Frémont, John C., 8

Great Basin, 33, 43

Hayes, Rutherford B. 47
Howard, Oliver, 40, 42

Malheur Reservation, 33, 36
Mann, Mary, 51
Modoc people, preparing for war, 33

Mud Lake Massacre, 26, 27

National Statuary Hall, 59
Nevada, 26, 27, 43, 45, 54, 55, 59
Numaga (cousin), 20

Ormsby Lizzie, 14
Ormsby Margaret, 14, 17
Ormsby, William, 14, 16, 17

Paiutes, Northern, 8; attack of white settlers, 26; in Bannock camp, 39–40; causes of death, 27, 28; conflict with white settlers, 19–20, 32; death from cholera, 12; escape from camp, 42; hunting and gathering, 18, 26; living conditions, 18–19, 23, 26, 27, 32; return to Pyramid Lake, 54–55; warriors, 25, 26, 28; way of life, 17–18; and Yakima Reservation, 42–43, 49, 50
Parrish, Sam, 34–36
Peabody, Elizabeth, 51, 55, 57, 58
Peabody Institute, 57
Pyramid Lake, 16, 20
Pyramid Lake Reservation, 27, 32, 33, 34
Pyramid Lake War of 1860, 20

"rag friend," 8, 21, 39, 51
reservation agents, 27, 28, 32, 33, 34, 36

Sarah's brothers, 7, 26
Sarah's mother, 8, 9, 10, 26
Schurz, Carl, 47, 49
Scott, Hiram, 10
Shoshone people, 27
Steens Moutain, 39, 40

Thocmetony, 59

U.S. Army, 20, 28, 38–39

Washo people, 16–17
white settlers, 7, 8, 12, 13, 16,
    23, 36, 49
Winnemucca, Chief (father), 8;
    at Camp Harney, 33; meeting
    with military, 33; perfor-
    mance, 23, 25; pleading for
    peace, 36; as prisoner, 39, 40;
    in retreat to Oregon, 27; in
    Washington, D.C. , 47
Winnemucca, Elma (sister), 14,
    17, 22, 58
Winnemucca, Lee (half
    brother), 34, 39, 40
Winnemucca, Mary (sister), 18, 26
Winnemucca, Mattie (half
    sister-in-law), 42
Winnemucca, Natches (brother),
    16, 27, 28, 33, 36, 38, 39, 45,
    47, 50, 53, 55, 58
Winnemucca, Sarah:
    as army scout and guide,
    38–42; autobiography of, 27,
    51; childhood, 7–17; death

of, 58; deceived by government, 42–43, 49; eastern trip,
50–51; education, 14, 18, 19,
22; at Fort Vancouver, 50;
gets "rag friend," 39; joining
activities, 18, 32; language
skills,14, 17, 18, 19, 22, 27,
28; living on ranch, 10; mak-
ing enemies, 32; meeting
with army officers, 28, 33;
move to Camp McDermit,
28; news stories about, 26,
27, 47, 49; opens school, 55,
57; with Ormsby family,
14–17; Paiute Princess, 18; as
peacemaker, 33; 33; plans
Paiute escape, 40, 42; published letter, 31–32; reaction
to white justice, 17, 27; and
reservations, 27, 32; role as
speaker, 25, 33, 45, 50; skills,
14, 22–23; statue of, 59–60;
as teacher, 34, 36, 45; as
translator, 23, 28, 34; trip to
California, 7–10; in Virginia
City, 23; in Washington,
D.C., 47, 52; working at
Malheur Reservation, 34–36;
at Yakima Reservation, 44, 49
Winnemucca, Tom, 33

Yakima people, 44
Yakima Reservation, 42, 43,
    49–50

About the Author

Jodie Shull is a former elementary school librarian and English as a Second Language teacher. She worked for a historic small town newspaper in western Nevada while her children were young. Now she lives within walking distance of the ocean in Carlsbad, California. Shull also wrote *Words of Promise: A Story about James Weldon Johnson*, another Creative Minds title.

About the Illustrator

Keith Birdsong is a self-taught illustrator from Muskogee, Oklahoma. He is part Creek and part Cherokee. Birdsong illustrated the five "Indian Dances" commemorative postage stamps issued in 1996 and the Martin Luther King "I Have a Dream" stamp, which is displayed in the Smithsonian Museum exhibit Art of the Stamp. He has also illustrated other stamps, several novels, collectors' plates, and posters.